The Art of Positive Thinking

A step-by-step guide to Emotional
Intelligence - How to control your negative
thoughts, achieve mindfulness and realise
your dreams incl. Self-Love and Self-
Acceptance

George Green

Table of Contents

Chapter 1
How to use this book

"Attitude is a choice. Happiness is a choice. Optimism is a choice. Kindness is a choice. Giving is a choice. Respect is a choice. Whatever choice you make makes you. Choose wisely."

Roy T. Bennett

Introduction

I know you may be saying that you have heard this all before. That thinking positively is necessary for happiness in your life and much better than being pessimistic. Many think that this was only achievable for the special ones and that changing is very difficult and not very scientific at all.

However, research shows that positive thinking does have a scientific basis, and though you may not be able to change the world, you can change how you view it and how you ultimately react to it. That, in its own way, can change the way that you feel about yourself and others, which can, in turn, have an insightful effect on your own wellbeing.

This book will take you through techniques and offer tips to help you see that the pathway forward for you is long term happiness, and you can achieve that. You will also learn how to stop negative thinking and relieve stress whilst generating more positivity and allowing you to close in on success and achievement.

Using techniques from masters worldwide and utilising these effective techniques, this book will recharge how you see and what you are doing with your life right now. The book will become your go-to 'bible' for topics that will give you a list of advice and techniques to help you along the way in a well laid out and easy to follow method/process. Because everyone learns and digests information differently, we have made this an excellent book to cater to all needs.

Each chapter will have significant ideas to put you into the subject's environment. This could be in the shape of a short story or real-life examples from real people, but always with tips and advice along the way.

The tips are handy to take in, as are the exercises. If you have a goal to be more positive and happier in life, I urge you to attempt as many activities as possible. Some are only short 10-minute exercises, others more prolonged, but the point you will never know if they work for you unless you actually try them!

This is what you will see at the end of each chapter to help you summarise and also take action:

Tip	Exercise
1	1
2	2
3	3

Before we get stuck in, lets us reflect on something that we all need to get done, respect ourselves and be happy. Responsibility.

Ultimately, You are responsible for everything that occurs in your life

Back in the 1800s, a boy was born into a rich family. Right from the start, the boy suffered severe health issues: an eye problem that left him temporarily blinded, a terrible stomach condition that forced him onto a strict diet, and back pains that would plague him throughout his life.

Despite his father's aspirations, he wanted to be an acknowledged painter when he grew up. His brother became known as a world-renowned writer, so there were brains in the family! As he entered adult years, much of his health problems worsened, his partnership with his father fell apart, and the young man began to deal with serious bouts of depression as well as self-destructive thoughts.

To fix his son's struggles, his father used his business connections to get his son admitted to Harvard Medical School. Fortunately, the young man was smart. He could handle the coursework. But he never felt at home or comfortable at Harvard. After touring a psychiatric ward one day, the young man wrote in his diary that he thought that he was more like the inmates rather than his fellow doctoral students.

Unhappy with his medical training, the young man looked for other academic opportunities that might suit him. He was desperate and was willing to try anything, even something radical and completely different.

Then he found an opportunity to travel to Brazil and the Amazon rainforest. The young man applied for this, excited to get away and start afresh, to perhaps learn something new and exciting about the world and himself.

In those days, intercontinental travel was long, difficult as well as dangerous. Many months later the young man made it to the Amazon. There he quickly caught smallpox and nearly died all alone in the jungle. He was rushed back to civilisation, and the expedition left him behind. On getting better from smallpox, his back spasms returned far more painfully than ever before. He was torn by the disease, stuck in a foreign land alone with no way to talk to anyone, and continuing to exist in daily excruciating pain.

The man managed to return home to a disappointed father, nearly 30 years old, still unemployed, a failure at everything he had ever tried, with a body that had given up on him and was not likely ever to get better. Regardless of every benefit as well as the possibility he had been given in life, he had failed them all. The only reality in his life seemed to be experiencing disappointment. The man fell into deep anxiety and intended to take his own life.

Yet first, he had a concept.

He agreed and made a pact with himself. In his journal, he created that he would attempt an experiment on himself. He would certainly spend one whole year believing that he was 100% in charge of every little thing that happened in his life, whatever. Throughout this period, he would certainly do everything in his power to transform his scenarios, no matter the outcome. If, he composed, at the end of one year of taking full obligation for whatever in his life and also working to boost it, if absolutely nothing in his life had actually improved within this time, then it was certain and apparent that he was genuinely vulnerable to any and all negative scenarios around him. And afterwards, should this be the case, he would take his very own life.

The boy's name was William James, a leader of American psychology as well as one of the most influential theorists of the past 100 years.

There is a realisation from which all potential personal growth emerges. This is the realisation that you are responsible for everything you do in your life, no matter the external circumstances.

In 1879, fifteen years after negotiating with himself, William James gave what was probably his most renowned lecture, labelled "The Will to Believe".

He said that whether religious or atheist, plutocrat or communist, everyone is compelled to adopt worth or some degree of faith. Even if you do not believe in religious celebrations/prayers, that is itself a true value requiring dedication. He went on to state that if we all have to value something, then we may as well learn and pursue the issue (s) that are most helpful for us and also others to overcome.

When we come to be in charge of our worth, we no more have to struggle to make the globe and people around us conform to our requirements; instead, we can adjust our worth to fit the scenarios that face us in the world.

It is that straightforward choice to take responsibility for ourselves as well as our own worth that allows us to control what occurs to us.

It permits us to change our adverse experiences right into encouraging experiences. It is totally counterintuitive – the idea that being responsible for all of the dreadful bad luck that befell us might somehow free us from them - yet it is true. Our obligation for ourselves releases a much deeper fulfilment by allowing us to take whatever we confront right into a worth that fulfils our demands.

Unruly children provide us the possibility and opportunity to be good mothers and fathers and also to teach some good manners. Ending up being jobless presents us the chance to explore brand-new occupation courses that we always fantasised about. A dreadful breakup enables us to take a truthful look at ourselves as well as how our behaviour affects our relationships with loved ones.

Undoubtedly, these experiences still hurt. Yet adverse experiences belong to life. The concern is not whether or not we have them, yet what we do when we are finished with them. Responsibility allows us to utilise our discomfort for empowerment, to alter our pain right into toughness, our loss into a possibility.

James was not foolish, though. He knew that values need more than a basic option or feeling to believe them. You do not just wake up one day and decide that I am a satisfied and effective individual and suddenly become it. Worth has to be cultivated, purposely tried and also tested and steeled by experience. Values wear out if they do not have real-world symptoms, some substantial advantage in a favourable experience.

We do not constantly regulate what happens to us. However, we still preserve a) exactly how we analyse what occurs to us as well as b) exactly how we respond to what occurs to us. Therefore, whether we knowingly identify it or otherwise, we are constantly in charge of our experiences. Picking not deliberately to translate events in our lives is still an interpretation of our lives' events.

Like it or not, we are constantly taking an energetic duty in what is accompanying ourselves. We are still analysing the significance of every minute and also every occurrence. We are constantly producing values about ourselves and also others. And we are always picking our actions based on those worth. Always.

Whether we know it or otherwise, we are already choosing our activities. We are already responsible for our adverse experiences. We just are not always mindful of it.

Time to be more conscious.

Time to make a difference.

Time to get positive!

Chapter 2

Know Thyself – Why You Need

to Be a Positive Thinker

"An unexamined life is not worth living."

Plato

We were born into this world with an open book, no preconceptions and love in our hearts and soul.

Our minds were clear and beautiful, yet open to the subtlest impressions. We had only taken what living in the womb had given us into the physical world that we found ourselves in at birth.

As time passed, we unknowingly created our self-sabotaging programmes, limiting belief structures and an ego that wanted to control us. Then we built up our defences against our authentic self and started to wear our mask daily.

The mask that we thought others wanted to see us wearing. To be accepted. To be wanted. To be loved. I always say that we go through our lives with two masks. The mask that is our authentic self, warts and all, and the second mask we wear because we want others to see us in that way. The trick is only to wear mask one – our true authentic self.

We slowly but surely got ruled by what we saw on TV, read in magazines, and witnessed in other people, mostly what our parents and teachers at school exhibited. We allowed these engrained perceptions to shape our understanding of who we think we are today. And you know what? We still enable others - a parent, spouse, teacher, manager, to say who we are.

Aware that we have a finite time on this planet, we start to ask ourselves: Who am I? Why am I here? Where am I going? Do I live my life on my own terms or someone else's? Do I live my life simply to please others?

Can I motivate myself?

You will never resolve these questions or life issues if you do not first **know yourself.**

For millennia, philosophers have questioned the very purpose of life; devotees have endured long and sometimes weary months in worship and solitude; travellers have trekked across the lands, soaking in cultures and aligning themselves with inner spirituality; still, others have taken to historical study, sifting through the centuries, separating fact from fiction in an attempt to gain the ultimate universal awareness to understand themselves.

However, it does not take a philosopher to question oneself about your worth in the universe. We can do it ourselves with some techniques that everyone can do.

First of all, though:

How do those BIG questions make you feel?

Do I live my life simply to please others?

You might experience an overwhelming urge to answer these questions right away. *Like you do know the answers.*

Indeed, you might think about these questions daily.

Or, you might have never thought about them – until this point.

You may also feel that you are truly missing out on something at the core of your existence.

According to psychotherapist Mel Schwartz, these questions often carry a sense of inadequacy along with them. When striving to understand who you indeed are, you might come across emotions ranging from emptiness, incompleteness, vulnerability to feelings of anger and self-doubt. Have no doubt, and there are advantages and disadvantages to getting to know yourself – the good, the bad and the downright weird!

So, to start with understanding yourself, you need to ask a fundamental question:

Are you content with your life?

Being content is possibly one of the most challenging emotions/feelings to achieve on a full-time basis. Many of us are simply not content with our lot.

Alternatively, imagine yourself dead the very next day. How does this make you feel? Content, relieved? Or unfulfilled, incomplete? How would you imagine those closest to you would react?

These answers will allow you to understand whether you are *content* with life as it currently stands. If not, apart from learning who you might be, it will focus your energies on receiving the help and guidance you need to be a more satisfied, complete individual.

Finding out who you are is the key and core to achieving the confidence, comfort, peace, and strength to *love* your life.

So, let us look at some techniques to help:

What makes you unique?

Allow yourself to sit down and construct a master-list of every nuance your personality possesses. Take this to be your brag-sheet of sorts, and genuinely pen down any unique skills, traits, or distinctive qualities of yours.

For instance, can you sing, write well, play the guitar or tap-dance? Are you incredibly skilled with budgeting, dancing, or memorising bits of trivia? Are you the comedian of your group of friends, or can you bake a mean cake? Are you creative or pragmatic? Was there ever an achievement that brought you immense pride? Or is your taste in music, books, movies, or fashion quite distinctive?

This list will stand as a *physical* collection of what you can individually offer. More often than not, referring to such plans dramatically impacts how we feel when faced with low self-esteem. In other words, it is good to look at this list when we need to remind ourselves just how good we really are!

Start journaling

One of the strongest ways to get to know yourself is through journaling (writing).

Journaling is an ancient tradition that dates back to at least 10th century Japan and perhaps even before that in Near East Arabic cultures.

Successful people throughout history have kept journals. Even rulers and presidents have maintained them for legacy reasons, other famous figures for their purposes. Oscar Wilde, the 19th-century playwright, said: "I never travel without my diary. One should always have something sensational to read on the train."

Journaling helps you connect to your inner wisdom, which is especially important in our noisy world.

You need to find the time (only 5-10 minutes in your day is not too much to ask, is it?) and get to somewhere quiet in order to start writing. By writing, I mean using the pages and the ink to express how you are feeling or events that might be affecting you in a way, both positive and negative. You should now and then look back at what you have written as a reminder and perspective about you – the real you.

Solitude

Being alone for a while in our lives can be a real eye-opener on finding out who we are. For some, being in solitude means cutting themselves away from everything and everybody for days on end. For others, it is the ability to do the same for hours rather than days. Whichever you choose to do, here are some of the benefits that solitude has in helping to know ourselves:

- Opportunity to self-examine yourself.

- Opportunity to enhance your relationships with loved ones in return.

- Allows the brain to reboot and unwind.

- Opportunity to think deeply.

- Opportunity to detox on food & drink items.

In Chapter 8, I will explain the Power of Solitude and all the good that time away can give to you.

Stop intense social media

Life in the current age is of a heavily publicised nature; with social media becoming part and parcel of the digital-age experience, it is quite common to begin and end your days scrolling through social feeds and witnessing glimpses into glamorous lives, exotic vacations and self-fulfilled smiles.

However, it is crucial to understand that the very same snapshots are intensely manicured, and the filters process far more than a bright face. Bordering on near-obsessive, we often find the need to create a perfect existence for ourselves online – often to compensate for feelings of emptiness and inadequacy in our physical reality.

Reducing the impact that social media might have on you will allow you to know yourself better. Try it and miss out on the daily fix of Facebook, Twitter and the like.

Getting to know yourself is not as difficult as it might appear. It is a journey for sure, but one well worth conducting. After all, why should we allow others to know us better than we know ourselves!

With the right attitude, we experience pleasant and happy feelings. This will brings brightness to the eyes, more energy and more happiness. Our whole being broadcasts the right choice, happiness and success.

This behaviour affects our physical, emotional and mental health in a beneficial way. Our body language exhibits the way we feel, whether we walk tall, and we speak more confidently. Positive and negative thinking are contagious. If you spend time around a person who is always pessimistic and moaning, you will suck their energy and take on their moans and groans. A big lesson here is to surround yourself with positive people and not the naysayers.

Identifying Negativity and Negative Thoughts

We probably all have negative thoughts or gloomy days, where everything seems to be either against us or deliberately brings us down. Negative reviews are associated with negative feelings such as sadness, anxiety, anger and hopelessness. We are often not aware of our negative thoughts as they often occur automatically, seem reasonable, and most of the time, believable. The more negative we feel about things, the more likely we are to think negatively and believe these thoughts to be accurate, even though they are unreasonable and unrealistic. It is a never-ending spiral downwards. Negative reviews are experienced by all of us but are more prevalent and extreme whenever we feel stressed, anxious, irritable or depressed.

Signs that negative thinking is running (and ruining) how you live your life:

If anything below resonates strongly with you, then there is a good chance you are a negative thinking person:

- life seems a constant struggle.

- you are convinced that everyone else is happier than you are.

- you have difficulty getting things done and finding your goals.

- you often stop yourself from doing the things you want to do.

- you think the world is a dangerous place.

- you end up feeling poorly of most people you get involved with.

- you have been told by those close to you that are a pessimist.

- you have issues with most of your co-workers and family members.

- you sabotage your success.

- you always feel stressed and anxious.

How can I stop negative thinking?

Try mindfulness

The trouble with negative attitude is that it can happen so quickly, as well as be such an ingrained routine, that we are not consciously familiar with how large the problem is. This is where mindfulness aids, and we will certainly cover even more of that in Chapter 6. It is about discovering to take notice of just how you assume as well as feel in each moment, and also with a method, you will find you can catch your ideas and choose how to transform them.

Practise self-compassion

The overall art of being nice to yourself, known as self-compassion, can be one of the quickest ways to self-esteem as it involves accepting yourself as is. And the more you take on your humanity, the more likely you are to accept it in others. Joining self-compassion with mindfulness can be very helpful. When you catch your negative thoughts, you can then replace them with kinder ones until, eventually, the more considerate ideas come naturally. We cover self-love also in Chapter 6.

Ask yourself a question

When you sense or know that you are having a negative thought or feeling about someone or somebody, a great way to counter this is to ask the question: "Who does this belong to? If you feel heavy when saying this, it does likely belong to you, and you can then ask yourself, "What can I do more of to move away from this feeling/thought". If, however, you feel light, then the chances are that this does not belong to you and that you can simply state, "Go Away feeling/thought, I have no time for you". It is incredible how this does work – you are challenging your subconscious questions that require answering and answers you will get!

Summary of Tips and Exercises

Tip	Exercise
1. You are unique – believe it, and it will be so.	1 – Sit down in a quiet place and compile a list of things that you believe make you great. For example, think of all those things you do that make you proud.
2. Start writing.	2 – Get yourself a small book or diary and make an effort every day to write something about how the day went. You only need to spend a few minutes or so but do it regularly. Writing in a journal can help relieve stress and anxiety, primarily if you focus on the positives.
3. Spend time alone.	3 – If you have the chance, try and spend some time on your own and examine how you feel. Sit under a tree and watch nature and realise how special it is and your connection with it.

4. Take a break from social media.	4 – Leave your phone at home for a short walk, stop using your computer in the evening, put your phone on mute to avoid the temptation of using social media.

Chapter 3

Building your Mental

Toughness

"Champions aren't made in the gym. Champions are made from something they have deep inside them – a desire, a dream, a vision. They have to have the skill and the will. But the will must be stronger than the skill."

Muhammad Ali

How to teach your mind to be positive – just tell your brain what you want

Here is a story that I often use in my leadership training as part of the 'knowing thyself module (you may have already heard of this story, but a reminder is always blessed):

An old Indian wizened in age is educating his grandson concerning life in general. "A fight is happening inside me", he claimed to the young boy.

"It is an awful fight between 2 wolves. One is evil – he represents anger, envy, sadness, regret, greed, arrogance, self-pity, regret, bitterness, inferiority, lies, incorrect satisfaction, prevalence, and ego".

He continued, "On the other hand there is the other wolf, who is good - he is pleasure, peace, love, hope, peacefulness, humbleness, kindness, generosity, empathy generosity, truth, empathy, and confidence. The same struggle is going on inside you, and inside every other person, too".

The grandson thought about it for a minute and
asked his grandpa, "Which one will win?".
The old Indian merely replied,
"The one you feed".

What a wonderful message for us, the key one being that whatever we tell our brain will manifest in front of us.

Why is it that some of us live up to our potential while others do not?

These are exciting questions, and there are no blanket answers. It would be naive to reduce the complexity of different people and their circumstances down to a singular and easy solution. Still, let us delve a little deeper. Let us see things like genetic differences and general luck factors and pretend that we have two people with similar ambitions, similar opportunities, and matching skills. Will they both be equally effective in life?

The answer is usually no. There is something more, and the biggest differentiator between those who get what they want and those who do not have a lack of determination, willpower, mental resilience and motivation are all terms commonly associated with the success of any kind. Much of the recent research has come to that conclusion, and broadly speaking, these things matter quite a bit, but not wholly so.

In different contexts, they may mean other things, but overall, being able to harness each of them comes down to one thing–the ability to control your mind and align it with what you need to do.

There are no shortcuts to do this, and I am not going to pretend to provide one. Still, fundamentally, a simple mental habit will give you a disproportionally large return on your investment of time and overall happiness if mastered.

But first, let us look at why controlling your mind is so tricky to begin with.

The Mental Battle

Most of the psychological issues we face can be attributed to a single conflict.

We have two prominent and largely opposed parts to our brains. An old reptilian part that was programmed to help us survive and reproduce in harsh and varied climates thousands and thousands of years ago and a modern element allows us to operate in a world suited for longer-term thinking.

The reptilian brain is incredibly efficient, and it is rapid to respond to stressors in our environment. That is where it primarily takes its cues from. It is emotional, and it enables us to stay in motion without thinking.

The modern brain is less efficient but more calculated. It takes its time and deliberates in evaluating our surrounding circumstances before it decides to act. It takes its cues from the rational mind before it responds.

By default, the reptilian brain is in charge. It lets us to operate on autopilot, and it requires less effort than deliberate thinking and planning.

However, to exercise control over your mind to get it to do what you need to do, you often need to put the modern brain at the helm. That is what will guide you to take on short-term disappointments (pain) to meet your long-term goals. That is how grit, determination, willpower and motivation are harnessed. But if the reptilian brain is in charge, what can we do to inspire the modern brain to take control consistently? The answer is practice, practice, practice.

A Simple Question

The primary driver of the reptilian brain is your environment. It sees the cues in your surroundings, and it then follows a comfortable pattern. The modern brain, on the other hand, has to be driven proactively. It has to be called upon. It positively can be influenced by your surroundings, but only if something out of the ordinary occurs. Otherwise, it takes the backseat and is unwilling to act. Many of us, have easy distractions in our environment, guide our minds into reactive behaviour to stop us from doing what we always need to do. A temporary solution would be to remove those distractions.

Over the long-term, however, you want more than that. You want to resist things not because they are there but because you have the mental control to do so. The following question comes in: *"Am I mindlessly reactive or am I proactive"*.

Next time you start to procrastinate, ask yourself this question. Next time you begin to feel unhappy, ask yourself this question. Next time you think of prematurely quitting on something, ask yourself this question. *"Am I mindlessly reactive or am I proactive"*.

Almost every time, you will feel your initial response is reactive. Something in your environment nudges you into these feelings, and they catch on.

When you make a repetition of asking yourself this question, however, you stop and pause right before you dive into the spiral of despair. It will not always inspire you to change your behaviour suddenly, but when you acknowledge that you are reactive, you can choose to either stick with it or not.

Most of the time, you will take control and think purposefully and nudge yourself towards the desired behaviour. Sometimes, you will stay where you are. Either way, you activate a part of the modern brain to make a deliberate choice, you practice a sense of control over your mind. Even just a feeling of power is one of the biggest motivators to be better. If you make this a habit, over time, you will also see quite substantial results.

Which Will It Be?

When you are reactive, your environment decides for you.

When you are proactive, you get to decide because you are in control.

A reactive person lets the world shape the outcome of their life. A proactive person takes the world as it is and shapes it into the world they want.

If you can successfully train your brain to deliberately question the state of mind and use that question to give you more control, you can do almost anything. You can quite literally reprogramme yourself.

This is not a quick route, and it will not happen overnight, but with one small step at a time, you can slowly align your mind-flex (mindset) with your potential.

The choice is yours. Get feeding the excellent wolf.

The overall benefits of mental toughness

This is why you would want to build mental toughness:

- conquers self-doubt.

- keeps you motivated, inspired to achieve and have success.

- helps you tune out unhelpful advice.

- you will learn from your mistakes and acknowledge them.

- provides courage to face your fears.

- helps you in bouncing back from failure.

- enables you to regulate your emotions.

Summary of Tips and Exercises

Tip	Exercise
1. Avoid procrastination, negative thought patterns.	1 – Ask yourself the question: "Am I mindlessly reactive or am I proactive."
2. Build your mental toughness or resilience.	2 – One step at a time. Walk taller (literally), acknowledge mistakes, listen to favourite music, try affirmations (Chapter 7), and surround yourself with positive people.
3. Build your mental toughness or resilience.	3 – Start examining who you are and what you want to achieve. If it is merely to feel better, do those things you enjoy most, like a walk-in nature or cooking a great meal. Build confidence daily until it becomes a habit.

Chapter 4

The Amazing World of

Emotional Intelligence

"Too often we underestimate the power of a touch, a smile, a kind word, a listening ear, an honest compliment, or the smallest act of caring, all of which have the potential to turn a life around."
Leo Buscaglia

First of all, what is Emotional Intelligence? This from Wikipedia:

Emotional intelligence (EI), **emotional quotient (EQ)** and **emotional intelligence quotient (EIQ)** s the capability of individuals to see and understand their own emotions and those of others, discern between different feelings and label them appropriately, use information to guide thinking and behaviour, and adjust emotions to adapt to environments. Although the term first appeared in 1964, it gained popularity in the 1995 best-selling book Emotional Intelligence written by science journalist Daniel Goleman. Goleman defined EI as the array of skills and characteristics that drive leadership performance. If you like, this was the forerunner to the term that we will look at later: *mindfulness.*

Essentially, EI means being *aware* of what is around you and what *part* you play in what is happening around you.

Five elements define EI, and they are:

- Self-awareness.

- Self-regulation.

- Motivation.

- Empathy.

- Social skills.

Let us look at what those mean:

Self-Awareness. Self-awareness is understanding your feelings and motives. Mentally intelligent individuals commonly show a high level of self-awareness. You understand just how your emotions impact yourself and others, and also you do not enable your feelings to regulate you.

Self-Regulation. People with the capacity to self-regulate do not make impulsive choices. You stop briefly and think about the repercussions of an action before continuing.

Motivation. People with psychological knowledge are effective as well as driven. You think of the big picture as well as analyse how your actions will certainly contribute to long-term success.

Empathy. Emotionally smart people are less most likely to be self-centred. Rather, you empathise with others and your situation. You have a tendency to be a good audience (listener), slow to judge, and also recognise others' needs and wants. For this reason, a mentally intelligent individual is typically seen as a devoted, caring close friend.

Social Skills. It is much easier for you to collaborate and work in teams. You often tend to be an exceptional leader as a result of your solid interaction skills and also ability to manage relationships. As a specific action, talk with others, pay attention to others and enjoy the business of others and what they are doing.

Some emotionally intelligent people do not realise this trait in themselves. So, this question still remains: What does emotional intelligence really look like? Here are a few indicators that could indicate those among us that display emotional intelligence:

- can be an excellent listener.

- not afraid to be vulnerable and share your feelings.

- understand your actions and behaviours that might affect others.

- happy to ask open-ended questions.

- able to shrug off a wrong moment and move on.

- viewed as an empathetic person by others.

- excellent problem solver.

- set boundaries and not afraid to say no.

- can get along with people in different situations.

- can accept constructive criticism without making excuses or blaming others.

- not afraid to admit your mistakes and apologise.

- self-motivated.

Understanding and avoiding anxiety

Anxiety is one of the most disturbing emotions that people feel. It is sometimes called fear or nervousness. The word anxiety describes several problems, including phobias that is fear specific things or situations such as heights, elevators, insects, flying in aeroplanes, panic attacks that can be intense feelings of anxiety in which people often feel that they are about to die or go crazy (post-traumatic stress order are repeated memories of awful traumas with high levels of distress), obsessive-compulsive disorder thinking about or doing things over and over again, and generalised anxiety disorder that we experience when faced with difficult experiences in our life.

Most anxious people are very aware of the physical symptoms, including jitteriness, tension, sweaty palms, light-headedness, difficulty in breathing, increased heart rate, and flushed cheeks. Anxiety is similar to depression in that the symptoms are experienced all over the human frame.

Significant events in our life and the environment we live in can contribute to anxiety. Examples of significant events leading to pressure are something that we call trauma, for example, being physically or sexually abused or being in a car accident or being in war (this would include non-combatants as well), illness or death, and things that we were taught when we were young, like snakes will bite you, or if you get dirty, you will get sick. The list is endless and can even include things we observe in an article in a newspaper about a plane crash or a local disaster like a factory explosion. Even experiences that seem too much to handle, like giving a public speech, perhaps a job promotion (and the additional responsibility that comes with it) or work termination and even having a new baby can lead to anxiety. I could go on.

All the physical, behavioural and thinking changes we experience when we are anxious are part of the act anxiety response called "fight, flight or freeze". The three answers can be adaptive when we face danger, and to see how this is so, imagine now that you are out of town. You decide to go for a walk in the evening and find yourself lost on a dark street. You notice a big man approximately 20 yards away walking towards you. You believe he sees you, and you think that he will attack and possibly rob you. What should you do? One option would be to stop and fight. To do this, your heart would start to pump faster, your breathing would speed up and your muscles would tense up ready for the fight. Sweating would also occur to help cool your body. All these body changes would be rather good in this situation to prepare you for any potential incident. These changes make up the fight response.

Maybe you do not think fighting this person is a good idea. Perhaps it might be better to break and run. To run fast, you would need to have an accelerated heart rate, plenty of oxygen, muscle tension and sweat. To that end, the same physical changes that make up the fight response will also make up the flight response. You just use the extra energy to run rather than to stay and do battle. With a little luck, running may save you from being attacked.

The "freeze" option is probably the worst of all. Lack of a decision or pure dread and fear can make us stop in our tracks, not knowing whether to go forwards, backwards, left or right. The anxiety levels rise for sure, with an increased heart rate. We feel utterly helpless and, as a result, do nothing. So, the BIG question is, how do we lower anxiety?

Methods to lower anxiety

- **Take exercise** – Exercise is one of the most important things you can do to combat stress. It might seem contradictory but putting physical pressure on your body through exercise can relieve mental stress. The benefits are most substantial when you exercise regularly. Scientifically it has been shown that people who exercise regularly are less likely to experience anxiety than people who do not do any physical exercise at all. Activities such as walking or jogging but involving repetitive movements of large muscle groups can remarkably stress relieving.

- **Reduce your caffeine intake** – Caffeine is a stimulant found in coffee, tea, chocolate and energy drinks. High doses may and can increase anxiety. People have different levels for how much caffeine they can cope with. If you are aware that caffeine makes you anxious and a little 'wound up', consider cutting back. Although much research shows that coffee can be healthy in moderate amounts, it is not for everyone. In general terms, three or fewer cups per day is considered a moderate amount. Try organic decaffeinated tea as a change – you will be pleasantly surprised at how tasty they can be!

- **Journal –** One way to cope with stress is to write things down. While recording what you are stressed about is one approach, another is jotting down what you are grateful for. Gratitude can often relieve stress and anxiety by aligning your thoughts on your life. We cover appreciation and gratitude in more depth in Chapter 5.

- **Laugh –** It is hard to feel anxious when you are laughing. It is suitable for your health, and there are a few ways it may help relieve stress. You are reducing your stress response, getting rid of tension by relaxing your muscles. In the longer term, laughter can also help boost your immune system and mood. For more information and tips about the power of laughter, see Chapter 9.

- **Share –** sharing your anxiety with family and friends is yet another great way to reduce your levels of stress. I am not talking about nervous laughter around a subject, but a real, honest opening of your heart, and you can trust to talk to about your inner worries and anxiety will bring results.

- **Environmental mood** – this is another beautiful calming way to help with any anxiety. Find a quiet space in the house (even your bedroom will do) and light a candle. Scented ones (like Lavender, Rose or Vetiver) are particularly nice as the infused scent will also penetrate the nostrils and enhance/stimulate the brain to chill. Aromatic essential oils in a burner do the same thing as a candle, although with a candle, it is very hypnotic to watch the flame flickering gently.

Summary of Tips and Exercises

Tip	Exercise
1. Take exercise.	1 – Even a short walk will increase the serotine in your brain and allow the neurones to spark in your brain, bringing with a memory function of being in the right place.
2. Reduce Stimulants.	2 – Cut down on caffeine and alcohol. Take a break from these deliberately and see how you begin to feel, particularly when you first wake. You will feel more charged to take on the day's challenges. It works!
3. Start journaling.	3 – Get yourself a small diary and write physically with a pen to relieve how you found the day – both good and bad parts. This is much better than sitting at a computer to do it.

| 4. Laugh and Smile. | 4 – This may sound daft, but it does make a difference. The brain acknowledges this human instinct as something to enjoy; therefore, it latches onto laughter and wants to repeat it. |

Chapter 5

Practising Gratitude

A personal story to start the chapter on gratitude.

It was my birthday the other day. Another number to add to my personal life experience that we call time. And yes, although it is a bit of a cliché, it most certainly is only a number. But birthdays are unique, as they become a celebration of all that you have learnt during the previous year. Quite often, they are shared with family and loved ones, but that, of course, is not always the case for everyone. For me, this was special, as it was my twin sisters) 60th birthday, but I was blown away by the love and words that came my way.

Firstly, I was humbled that most of my birthday celebrations were organised by my three loving children. They gave up their time (a precious commodity for anyone) to mark this occasion for me and one that I will never forget.

Secondly, I received through the power of short video clips, messages from family and friends. These had an incredible effect on me as I listened to people's comments about me. I am not ashamed to say that my eyes welled up with tears throughout almost 30 minutes of playtime.

Thirdly, it was not just one evening of laughter and celebration – it took over two days, many activities (swinging in treetops as an example!) and a general fun time.

It then came over me like a wave – that I was so grateful for all the people that made my life. As I paused and looked around myself, I knew that it was me that should be saying beautiful things to all those beautiful souls smiling at me! A return of gratitude is a lesson that I have learned, but perhaps I do not express it as often as I should do – time to focus on that a bit more.

I also started to think more about taking a closer look at the tiny things that I might take for granted. So, everyone's message does not just focus on the big and obvious things you can be grateful for, it is very often the small things in life that we can be grateful for.

Think about what tiny things you are grateful for.

Like the flower in front of my laptop that I am writing these words on, it is not a remarkable plant. It has simple beauty in the vibrant purple colour, keeps growing, and the faint smell and sight of nature is something I am grateful to witness.

One aspect that I am grateful for today – that I often take for granted – was my breakfast. It was a beautiful smoothie made for me by my wife. It was delicious. And, more importantly, I do not have to go hungry. I am lucky to be able to eat breakfast every day. Not everyone around us has that.

Get Energised!

Have you seen people who exude enthusiasm and have a sparkle in their eyes? There is a look of contentment, decisiveness, and peace that you simply cannot ignore but just admire. These are individuals who follow their interests and loves, live a life of satisfaction, are highly motivated, and most of all are happy! They have made an effort to discover their interests, and they **do** something about it to make it an irreversible ingredient of their lives. To find these interests, you need to follow your heart and instincts and discover things that energise and influence you. Then make the best of it/them. Get energetic!

Do Everything with Love

Understand quickly that there is no point in doing things if there is no love behind them or at least some love. Everything we do should have a piece of love attached to it. We need to apply this to everything we do, from our work lives (how many of us love what we do?) to the somewhat mundane activities of life such as washing the car, shopping, taking a shower etc.; If you start thinking about the personal benefits you receive by doing these so-called mundane activities, you can soon learn to appreciate and love doing them. Anything you do should have a love connection with why you are doing it. Otherwise, do not do it!

Get in the Best Shape Feasible

We could spend forever going from one diet plan to another, buying gym subscriptions, looking at nutritional values and reviewing articles on the healthy way to conduct our lives. We could also buy supplements, fast for days, run hard - the list is endless. However, it is down to our **approach** to getting in the best shape possible and our **mental fortitude**. Without dedicating ourselves to getting fit, we will find it difficult to become successful in other sectors of our life or feel happy and completely satisfied as a whole. Healthy body = a healthy mind. It does not take much effort, even if you think you cannot or do not have the time. That is a lame excuse; decide to do it and set aside some time. Plan what you want to achieve, start small and also do something every day, no matter how little. Everyone can give 15 minutes per day!

Provide

When you have a lot to do in good and hard times, and have absolutely nothing, when you enjoy life and are depressed, keep in mind to be there for others. It is a small thing to do.

Life is absolutely nothing if we do not share, help and provide. There is a personal higher conscious of satisfaction, knowing that you have helped someone. It could be a small thing, but little things matter! Try random acts of kindness – they are fantastic for both the giver and receiver's well-being. When was the last time you saw someone help an older person across a busy road or offer to give someone a lift into town? Make it your goal to help someone, somewhere, at least once a week.

Challenge your Habits

Many of us are wired not to take too many risks – it is a human thing. However, a few out there enjoy taking that extra step or choose to do things differently, which in itself has an element of risk associated. And why not? Taking risks can be exciting and also hugely fulfilling. So, go out there and throw down the gauntlet to yourself whenever you have the opportunity. Daily, try something new, do something that frightens you (Baz Luhrmann encouraged us to do this in 1990 with his song!), amaze yourself and those that know you. This way, you will broaden and expand the limits you set yourself (unconscious and conscious limits). You will become a fascinating individual, prepared or preparing for new journeys that challenge and excite. Remember, our lives are not some special rehearsal; we need to live it now! Which leads nicely to the next point.

Living Now and Loving It

Living in the now, absolutely experiencing it and being grateful about it is a powerful feeling to have. It can help you focus on precisely what you have right now, a perspective that can alter your world. How often during your day do you look back at events that have happened, over which you have no control anymore? We may feel happy about something in the past or even sad – but guess what, we have no influence anymore on that event. What we can influence, however, is our now. Look at every minute as a beautiful opportunity to maybe complete that piece of work that you wanted to finish, relish the people around you or stare in awe at the planet that exists. View the stars, the moon, the sun, clouds, sky, forests and lakes with wonder – it is a beautiful way to excite your brain – try it out!

Enjoy Quiet

A pilot knows that if they fly into the centre of a hurricane, there is stillness and calm – yet all around them, the wind howls, and the storm rages. We live in busy and often noisy environments – hopefully not with too many hurricanes! However, establishing contact with yourself during quiet times is going into the centre. It is a beautiful connection to make and challenging to do. Find a room at home and shut the door and be in the stillness. You can walk into the fields or woods and sit down in a secluded spot. You will find the place, and then, you just need to do – nothing! Quieten your inner talk by staring at the sky, a flower, the flame of a candle, all guaranteed to allow escapism and quietness. Even sub - subconsciously, connecting to you, your soul purpose and wonderfully cleansing to do. Try this, and it is worth it just for 10 minutes of your daily life.

So, ask yourself:

- What is one tiny thing that I can be grateful for today?

- What is something I usually take for granted that I can be especially grateful for?

Opening your eyes to the small things every day that you can appreciate and allows you truly see more of the simple beauties in life.

To keep the gratitude 'kick' going is not always easy.

Two things that I have found useful and might work for you:

- Take just a minute in the morning to get an excellent start to your day by finding three small things you are thankful for and say them out loud.

- Take 1-2 minutes each evening and write in a journal 2 or 3 things that you are grateful for about the day you have just had, about yourself or your life.

Try one of these little exercises every day for a week and see how it impacts your life and remember to be grateful and express that.

Do not just keep the gratitude on the inside. Express it. Show it to others, and they too will pick up the baton and run with it.

Make other people happy, too, by showing how you are grateful for having them in your life. Additionally, their smile and the joy in their eyes when you tell them this will make you happier too. Words cost nothing but can have a lasting effect. I love the notion of random acts of kindness.

An excellent example of this would be walking through town, helping an older person cross the road. That seemed to be the norm in years gone by, but it appears to be less common nowadays. Or, if you have a neighbour who struggles with gardening, perhaps just knock on the door and say you will do an hour weeding for them. And guess what? Not only will you bring a ray of light into that person's life, but you will also feel loads better yourself for doing it! Little things do matter, so try them out!

So, tell the people in your life how grateful you are for them. And a promise to myself is not to leave expressing gratitude until the next birthday comes along.

Visualisation

Visualisation is a method of using your imagination to experience new behaviours or joy inside your head, which you can then offer to the outside world. For example, elite athletes in sports worldwide have been using visualisation techniques with great success for decades. Professional public speakers will also rehearse their presentations/talks many times before stepping out on the stage. Indeed, I have visited the place that I am due to do a conference in so that I can visualise where the audience will be, the entrance is, the lectern position on the stage etc.; this all helps and heightens my confidence come the time/day that I am to perform. I can just close my eyes and visualise the venue and imagine the audience. It is so cool!

Here are some of the benefits of visualisation:

- It can activate your subconscious, which generates creative ideas to help you achieve your goals.

- It will programme your brain to recognise and perceive resources that you will need to start achieving your dreams.

- It will activate the law of attraction, which will draw into your life the essential people and circumstances required to achieve your goals.

- It will build internal motivation and confidence.

Tibetan and Buddhist monks have been performing visualisation exercises for thousands of years to calm the mind and bring enlightenment for themselves and, by definition, to the world around them. Have a look at this 3,000-year-old Tibetan visualisation exercise:

This version of a 3,000-year-old exercise comes from the John Perkins book Shape-Shifting: Shamanic Techniques for Global and Personal Transformation.

It was given to John by a European traveller, who learned it from Tibetan sages. The sages told the traveller that it would most assuredly make dreams manifest.

Start by closing your eyes. Keep your eyes closed until you are totally completed. Now, envision your intention. Now imagine the black void of space all around you. Now picture a bright, shimmering star at a distance out in front of you. Push your intention through your third eye (which resides in the middle of the forehead) out to the shimmering silver star, where that silver star will then absorb it. Once that star has taken your intention, draw it containing your purpose into your mind through your third eye.

Now, the picture that the star-filled with your intention explodes three times in succession with your mind. These are transformational growth explosions. They are concentrating the power of your vision. Following these three growth explosions, direct the silver star containing your intention down into your heart.

Once again, imagine three powerful growth explosions in your heart. Finally, draw the silver star filled with your intention up and out of your third eye, back out into the black void.

Their advice would be to perform this exercise at least twice each day, three times per week. That could seem a little over the top, but the whole point here is that excellence and habit are good enough, and with repetition, we do prosper.

Summary of Tips and Exercises

Tip	Exercise
1. Be grateful every day.	1 – When you wake up every morning before getting out of bed, ask yourself two things: What can I do today to assist someone else? What three things am I grateful for today?
2. Do random acts of kindness.	2 – Make it your mission to do at least one random act of kindness this week and coming weeks. They can be small things and do not necessarily take much time – so help someone with something (you do not even need to know that person).

3. Start a daily visualisation process in your life to improve your optimism.

3 – Create the happiest place you could imagine and visualise that place daily. It can be somewhere you have been or an imaginary location that represents pure joy. Anyone or anything that you love can be present in this place. You should spend at least ten minutes merely soaking up the festive, stimulating atmosphere that you create.

Chapter 6

Mindfulness and its Power to Help You

"Mindfulness is a way of befriending ourselves and our experience"

Jo Kabat-Zinn

Mindfulness is a term that reached us perhaps 30 years ago and is now a well-used term. Mindfulness is a technique you can easily learn and involves making a special effort to notice what is occurring in the present moment (in your mind, body and surroundings) – without judging. It has foundations in Buddhism and meditation, but you do not have to be spiritual, or have any particular beliefs, to try it out.

It aims to help you:

- be kinder towards yourself.

- feel more able to select how to respond to your thoughts and feelings.

- become more self-aware.

- feel calmer and less stressed in moments.

- cope with negative or unhelpful thoughts.

Mindfulness Exercises

In this busy world, the mind is always pulling us, scattering our thoughts and emotions and leaving us feeling stressed, highly-strung and at times, quite nervous and anxious.

Most of us claim not to have five minutes to sit down and relax, let alone 30 minutes or more for a meditation session.

But it is essential for our well-being that a few minutes each day can cultivate mental spaciousness and achieve a positive mind-body balance.

You can use these simple exercises to empty your mind and find some much-needed calm.

I am going to cover five exercises that I learned many years ago on an NLP course which take minimal effort and can be done pretty much anywhere at any time:

Mindful hand awareness exercises

Get hold of both hands and grasp them tight and hold for 5 – 10 seconds, then let go and see how your hands feel. Keep your attention solely focused on the feeling for as long as you can.

Mental focus exercise

Sit comfortably and stare at any object and remain focused on that item for as long as possible. Keep a watch on when your mind starts to wander, then just bring it back to the item. The longer you can remain calm and objective, the more mindfulness will increase.

Musical stimuli exercise

Listen to your favourite song track and think about how it makes you feel. What memories come to mind, and how do those memories make you feel? Do you go back to when you first heard that music? Who was there?

How did you think? Engage in the emotions you are feeling and see where they lead.

Undivided attention exercise

Do something around the house that you have never done before and do it with utter and undivided attention. This might be cleaning the skirting board behind the sofa, picking up a plant and cleaning the leaves gently – anything that you would not normally do.

Full sensory awareness exercise

Wherever you are, just hold on and look around when it is safe to do so (not when you drive!). Become aware of all that your senses pick up. What are the eyes seeing? What noises (if any) can you detect? Is it cold or warm? How do you feel? Do you think over-stimulated? What can I smell? Do you feel warmth in your heart? Make a mental note and keep observing for up to 10 minutes.

Self-Love and Esteem

There are a lot of people walking along the streets of their life with a lack of self-esteem. Sometimes it is just for brief periods, say for a day or a week; for some, it is every day. I know because I have indeed suffered from periods of little or no confidence, little or no capability of making a decision, little or no evidence of really 'living in my skin'.

Papering over the cracks by pretending that things are okay is systematic with a lack of self-esteem. Here, displays of confidence, outwardly being an extrovert in social situations all mask your real feelings.

And here are some of the signs that you suffer a lack of self-esteem as identified by Glenn R. Schiraldi, PhD, author of The Self Esteem Workbook and a professor at the University of Maryland School of Public Health:

- Sensitivity to criticism.

- Withdrawing from social situations.

- Hostility.

- Excessive thoughts of personal problems.

- Physical symptoms such as tiredness, insomnia and headaches.

Recognise any of those in yourself? I certainly have seen some of these in me!

I met someone the other day that exhibited all of these signs – pretty much within 30 minutes! I decided to investigate a little more about what we can do to help ourselves move away from a lack of confidence and lack of self-esteem into a brighter and more confident you.

This what I found in the shape of small steps that are easy to achieve, and most importantly, actually work!

Gain Control of Yourself: Never be critical of yourself in front of others. It can be useful to let someone else know of your concerns to someone you trust, telling everyone you meet is something else. Be kind to yourself. Make a list of all of your good qualities; believe in yourself.

Do Not Be a Complainer: Everyone has problems, so why should yours be more significant than others? By being negative, you can shut yourself off from others and cut yourself off from solutions to questions.

Learn to Relax: Allow time each day for yourself. This may only be a short time, but it is essential to be quiet and to unwind. This does not have to be an organised meditation, but a quiet time anywhere you feel like – home, garden, park or on a hill.

Boost Your Morale: Allow yourself a treat from time to time. It does not have to be much - a cup of tea at a pleasant cafe, or some other pleasure, like buying a great book or going to the cinema.

Thank yourself for a job well done and even perhaps tell a friend. Do not be the one that always gives out praise, you need some too. Justified praise is an excellent morale boost. That old expression gives us a pat on the back, actually does you a lot of good – so hug yourself.

Learn to Channel Nerves and Tension Positively: when you are worried or nervous, adrenalin gets pumped around the frame. Additional energy can be used to good effect, enabling you to communicate with more tremendous enthusiasm and intensity.

Learn to be Assertive: Stand up for what you believe in and not be pressured by others. You do not have to be overly opinionated; just clear in what you think is right and not concerned about saying it!

Improvements will come in small steps.

It is difficult to go from low self-esteem to positive self-esteem overnight; instead, you will find you make small improvements over some time. Make an effort to try and stay in touch with how you feel during the day.

Do you feel good about yourself? Why is that? If you feel low and sense negative thoughts running through your mind, ask yourself why this is the case. Half the battle to conquering low self-esteem is to identify when and why you feel a certain way. If you find exercise is a large booster to you, you can build more of it into your day. If you feel low and you are on your own, make plans to get out and about more often, find solace in nature. You do not have to live with low self-esteem.

By taking positive steps towards solutions, you can start moving in the right direction and boost your self-esteem and love for yourself.

Summary of Tips and Exercises

Tip	Exercise
1. Try out the mindfulness exercises above.	1 – Every day, try out the following and see how you feel: Hand awareness. Mental focus. Musical stimuli. Undivided attention. Full sensory awareness. Give these exercises at least 10 minutes of your time and record how you felt – write it down in your journal!
2. Love yourself and increase your self-esteem.	2 – Love yourself: Make a list of all the great things you do. Try not to complain. Relax every day, perhaps in meditation or just quietly

somewhere in your home or outdoors.

Give yourself a treat of some description every day.

Use heightened feelings or adrenaline to your advantage.

Avoid saying yes when you actually mean no.

3. Daily check-ins.	3 – Throughout your day, check to see how you feel about specific scenarios as they appear. Always look for the positives and reassure yourself that you are doing the right thing.

Chapter 7

Meditation and Affirmations

"I sound to my soul, be still and wait without hope, for hope would be hope for the wrong thing; wait without love, for love would be the love of the wrong thing; there is yet faith, but the faith and the love are all in the waiting. Wait without thought, for you are not ready for thought: So, the darkness shall be the light, and the stillness the dancing."

S. Eliot

Humans have meditated since the beginning of time. This quiet space allows us to think deep within ourselves. Meditation is one of the best techniques we have to counter negative talk, release any accumulated stress that may have built up, foster positive experiences and intentions but most importantly, enjoy the peace of the present moment, in other words, the now. A large body of research has established that having a regular meditation practise produces tangible benefits for mental and physical health.

There are steps, and the best advice I could give would be to find someone who meditates regularly. They will know how to achieve a level of meditation and you in turn, can adopt and adapt. This is because everyone does it slightly differently, and I can only give you pointers to how I achieve peaceful mediation. There are two steps: preparation and mediation.

Preparation for Meditation

I started to work on a small preparation ritual for meditation. Of course, this may not work for you as we are all different (thankfully), but it helps me ready myself for reflection. Although I describe this for the outdoors, it can easily be adapted for indoors as well:

- Wait for the sun to shine or at least know the direction it is if hiding behind clouds.

- Expose your heart to the sun (chest out towards the sun).

- Take off your shoes and socks so that your feet feel the earth below.

- By doing this, you have grounded with Mother Earth through your feet' soles and open to the heavens above through your heart.

- Sit (or stand whichever you prefer) in a comfortable pose, back straight, legs apart, arms on your knees or to the side and look forward.

- Now breathe in through your nose and exhale through your mouth.

- Be aware of your breathe in and hold it when your lungs are comfortably full. Count to 3, then exhale slowly. Imagine with each breath that you fill every cell in your body with life-giving oxygen and the light from the heavens.

- Listen to your heart gradually slow to the tempo of your breath.

- After 5 minutes or so of gentle breathing, you have now prepared yourself for the next stage - meditation.

Meditation itself

To start meditating, get to a place where you are able to sit comfortably and quietly. As I indicated above, I chose to do this outdoors, but you may have a quiet place at home to have your meditation. The main thing is that you will be undisturbed. Close your eyes and do absolutely nothing for a minute or so. Thoughts may come to you during this time, and that is fine. Then start a piece of relaxing music – there are heaps of these you will find on the internet. It could be just the sound of rainfall or waves breaking on a shoreline. It may even involve singing bowls chiming in the background – whatever it is, and you will soon drift off into a mindful state whereby feelings. Thoughts and images may well come to you. If they do not, fear not, like many things in life, mediation does take practice. Just be and try not to force anything. A period of stillness will eventually come you, and you may even fall asleep!

Sometimes, attached to meditations are things we call affirmations. Affirmations help you chose your thoughts and the experiences you want from those thoughts. You should write them down and then speak them out loud or to yourself. They should be written in the positive and feel right for you. Here are a few examples:

- All of my desires are achievable.

- My life is full of unique possibilities.

- I am enthusiastic about what I can achieve.

- I respect and love myself.

- I commit to learning new things.

- I believe, trust and have confidence in myself.

The list is endless, and you will create your own to fit you and your environment.

What are Mantras? A mantra is a sound, word, or even a sentence used in constant repetition that helps in concentration or meditation on a specific topic. A mantra lulls the overactive mind and, in doing so, helps the user to focus on one particular thought or idea at a time. As you can see, they are very much used similarly to affirmations – the only difference I would say is that they could be used specifically for meditation, whereas affirmations can be used outside meditation – something you could repeat to yourself throughout the day. These are a few ideas for you to use:

- I am worthy.

- I love myself.

- I am free.

- I honour myself.

- I am the creator of my own future.

Summary of Tips and Exercises

Tip	Exercise
1. Meditate.	1 – Prepare yourself for a meditation session – utilise the steps outlined above.
	Find a quiet spot, close your eyes, repeat your mantra and just drift off.
	Try to repeat this every day, because practice makes perfect.

2. Affirmations.	2 – Make a list of all the affirmations that you believe fit you. The longer the list, the better, as writing them down will also enhance your self-esteem. Use them (one perhaps daily) and note how you feel.
3. Mantras.	3 – Mantras will be shorter than affirmations, and again, it will be useful to make a list of them. Once you have some, use them at the start of your mediation by repeating them repeatedly. The conscious brain will suck these up and implant them into your deeper subconscious.

Chapter 8

Exercise in Nature

*"Look deep into nature, and then you will understand
everything better."*
Albert Einstein

Hope, Health and Nature

In Greek mythology, Pandora was the first human
woman created by the gods. Zeus ordered her to be
shaped out of the earth as part of the punishment of
humanity for Prometheus' theft of the secret of fire.
According to the legend, Pandora opened a jar, in current
accounts often mistranslated as Pandora's box, releasing
all the evils that visit humanity like pain and suffering,
leaving only hope inside once she had closed it again. The
moral of the story was that despite all the evil out there
globally, there is still hope, so not all is lost.

And connecting with nature allows us to see hope, which in turn gives us hope. But not just hope, because being physically in nature also has undoubted health benefits.

In recent years, a lot of experimental studies have linked nature exposure with increased energy and a heightened sense of wellbeing. A good example is that research has shown that people on wilderness 'experiences' report feeling more energetic and that just bringing to mind outdoor experiences has increased happiness and health. I would 100% agree with that having spent two periods in solitude and always returned to the everyday world feeling more vitalised and calmer within myself.

Some other studies also suggest that the very presence of nature helps ward off exhaustion feelings and that 90% of people report increased energy when placed in outdoor activities.

People are more caring and generous when taken into nature. We have a natural connection with all living things. After all, nature is something within which we live and breathe, so having it be more a part of our lives is important, especially when we live and work in built environments and are buzzed the whole time with technology. The importance of having access to any natural surroundings and of bringing natural elements into our buildings through windows and indoor plants cannot be overstated or overlooked.

Now, a scientific study is documenting the overall impacts of nature on us flourishing—our social, psychological, and emotional life. Many studies have stated that being in nature, living in our heart, or even viewing wildlife in paintings and videos can positively impact our brains, bodies, feelings, thought processes and social interactions with others. In particular, viewing nature seems to be extremely rewarding, producing a waterfall of position emotions and calming our nervous systems. These, in turn, help us develop big openness, creativity, inspiration, connection, generosity, warmness and toughness.

Science suggests we may seek out the natural world not only for our real and physical survival but also because it is good for our social and personal wellbeing. Added to that, wellbeing induces awe, wonder, and reverence, all emotions known to have various benefits, promoting everything from wellbeing and enhanced health.

If there were one thing I would encourage you to do to get the full benefit from being in nature, it would be:

Grounding

Here is an extract from my solitude diaries to explain the importance and health benefits of genuinely grounding (sometimes referred to as earthing).

The feeling of cold water and fine sand on the toes and ankles was terrific! I had read once about the importance (and health benefits) of properly connecting with the earth by getting your shoes and socks off and exposing your naked feet to the ground.

The reason is quite simple.

Our planet has electrical currents running all over it, literally everywhere. There are some significant lines, and these were coined with the term Ley Line by Alfred Watkins in the 1920'ss, and these feed off the mega grid system that encompasses the whole of the earth. Think of it like B class roads leading to A-class roads and in turn up to the motorway system. Never mind the country paths, tracks, railways and airways as well! If we humans can connect via roads and railways, we are only copying the planetary communication lines laid down since the earth's birth.

These planetary energy lines are far more unique, though, as they directly link to Mother Earth or Gaia. The whole subject about the earth's energy lines would take an entire book to describe, be, and there are plenty of those out to read if you are interested. As far as I am concerned, it means to me being able to ground and enjoy the earth of the earth given to us free. I honestly believe that it is good for us both physically and spiritually to connect to those energy frequencies sent out from the world.

So, given a chance, get those shoes and socks off (an obstacle to connection) and walk around in your back garden, the local park or across fields with your bare feet and soles on the ground. You will love it!

Take in the environment around you as you escape the walls of your dwelling or home. It is beautiful to notice the small things and how perfect they are - tiny snails climbing baby fern shoots with beautifully formed spiral shells with the rain glistening on their bodies. The endless drifting flight of birds in the sky, making tiny changes on the wing to bring about an effortless change in direction.

This morning the sound of woodpeckers hammering at a branch, the arrival of yellow and green spotted toads around the lake and the beauty of old and ancient trees gave me a real boost.

Trees are frankly unique. They are marvels of nature, and some are still-standing giants of extraordinary longevity. We all know about the health benefits to the planet that they offer and give us, yet sometimes we just take them for granted. They help combat climate change by absorbing CO_2 and releasing oxygen back into the air. They clean the air by absorbing odours and pollutants (nitrogen oxides, ammonia, sulphur dioxide and ozone). They provide oxygen, for example, one care of mature trees can provide enough oxygen for 18 people. They help with soil erosion, give us shade and provide food and resting places for birds and wildlife. There are many more benefits.

But what I wanted to say was that you could wonderfully start the day by just looking at a tree and marvelling at its beauty. Even in these somewhat restrictive times, you might be able to see one in your garden, through a window, or even a photograph on your computer screen. Perhaps you will pass one on your daily exercise walk or run.

Looking at trees or spending time among them if you can and touching them can help positively centre your energy. Sharing a tree's beauty can be very healing and help you reconnect with the sacredness of life and all things alive. Here are some thoughts on working with trees.

Try physically hugging a tree. Visualise your scattered or negative energy travelling down the tree's roots to be recycled by Mother Earth. Now you can picture the tree absorbing nourishing energy from Mother Earth up through its roots and back to you. It is a return service.

Consider taking this a step forward by offering thanks to the tree (mentally or verbally) for helping you to ground your energy. When you this, you not only raise your positive vibrations and the trees, but you will also increase the planet's life. It is a lovely and straightforward spiritual and healing practice. And guess what? It works!

So, try it today, and thank the tree that you look at with gratitude, and it will be returned!

So why seek solitude?

"Whatever happens to the beast, also happens to the man.
All things are connected."
Chief Seattle, Suwamish Tribe

Unlike what can be termed as the negative state of loneliness, I think solitude is a favourable and useful experience of engagement with oneself. Seclusion is rejuvenating, a time of getting on your own where you voluntarily pull back from the firm of other individuals to find yourself.

Solitude is being alone without feeling lonely.

The beauty of undertaking solitude or "retreat", as was termed at my old school run by Carmelite priests, is the attitude towards us being alone. In seclusion, we delight in spending time alone due to the fact that we know and understand everything that we require to know in order to recognise our authentic self.

Solitude can be made use of to get fresh perspectives that enable us to appreciate those points that matter. Learning to be comfortable in your very own firm is an ability you can establish, which will substantially assist throughout your life. It is a genuine break from people, regardless about much we like them!

I believe that privacy is a crucial active ingredient to a healthy and balanced sense of self. It provides us with a committed time to find as well as to be familiar with ourselves much better. By being at the centre of our very own lives, we feel that we are back to the 'self', instead of being buffeted by outside forces at all times. When you consider it, we have so very seldom managed to be on our very own throughout our lives - might be to the level that we rely upon and require other people around or near to us. Yet in doing so, we are never able to understand ourselves as we continue to be affected by other people as well as their point of view.

With exterior stress on us ever-increasing in this hectic, 24-hour, interconnected world, we often desire a sense of equilibrium as well as self-assurance that we supervise or take charge of our very own lives. Not only do we seek to be in control of occasions, or at the very least understand them, likewise we want to know even more concerning ourselves as well as our destiny throughout our life. Otherwise, we can feel overloaded as well as strained by outside influences, and we never ever live the life that we wish to.

Besides, what anguish would there be at the end of our life with a realisation that we undoubtedly had not lived or got truly involved with all our energy and purpose?

Today, as never before, I recommend that many of us require to discover solitude. We are moving forwards into exciting times, although a lot of us do not understand that fact! The globe is transforming, albeit gradually, but altering it is.

Like a psychological and also spiritual thermostat, being alone provides us the ability to form as well as change our lives, it can instruct us how to have inner strength and also check out the larger picture, see our duty in it, rather than count on others to dictate what we must be doing.

Yet we have become reluctant and careful in seeking out seclusion as a result of our fear of solitude as well as not having access to all the features of the contemporary, fast-paced lives that we often tend to live.

Preparing for solitude

I thought it would be good to tell you of some of the needs to prepare in order to get ready for blast-off.

Unfortunately, very few of us can just go into solitude without some kind of getting ready for it. We have other people and commitments to think about before we can arrange a quality alone time away.

So, how did I get ready to go into solitude?

Readying my mind

At first, the idea of being all alone can make you feel a little nervous. If this is the case, take a little time to ask yourself why this is. It is helpful to think through the issues you have with being in your own company before creating a time of solitude. But do not let these doubts stop you from going on with your plans, you can always use your alone time to work through these issues.

For me, over the time I spent alone, I think you will most certainly bring up emotions and feelings about who you are and what you have done. Do not be afraid of this; it is a good thing; trust me! These emotions will undoubtedly come up in reflection and meditation and just walking in the day or preparing food in the evening. The thing is, you will get into a state where you will allow these feelings to come right up into the stark and honest forefront of your thinking and not be discarded as being too painful or silly to think about.

When most people think of solitude, they start to imagine the bitter pain of being alone. To many, the concept of aloneness evokes our deepest fears of abandonment and a lack of belonging. It can also be seen as boring.

However, loneliness is not merely a case of being alone – many people can be with people and still feel lonely. I think that loneliness is the belief that no one cares about what happens to us, and this is totally incorrect.

We may believe that it is the distressing realisation that we lack close and meaningful contact with others that, in turn, produces feelings of being completely detached from them.

It is this simple need to avoid being alone that drives us to create so many connections around ourselves. Our computers and mobile telephones reassure us by providing the tools to stay always in touch with each other. Yet, these electronic props only lead us away from listening to our internal voice and increasing our sense of self-awareness.

This obsession with staying tuned in to the outside means we forget how to contact our inner selves. I thought that I would not be worried by loneliness but was unpleasantly surprised halfway through my time away, with feelings of acute loneliness and sadness. Lonely, chiefly because I missed my family, but happily for me, it washed out after about 48 hours and did not return.

Deciding your time

Hopefully, you already have some me-time built into your life, even if it is just for a few hours every so often. The exact length of time you need depends on your situation, but it is essential to organise a dedicated period rather than just hoping you can grab a few hours here and there. The more quality time you can set aside, the better, although even just 1 hour session is better than nothing at all. The important factor is *how* you spend your time in solitude, not the minute, hours or days spent away.

So, what is a reasonable period? I think that everyone will have his or her feelings. I know that I found that it has taken me up to 7 days to settle in, so for me I always have to be away for at least a week or more. The longer the period, then definitely the more insights will be offered to you. What matters is that you locate somewhere you can enjoy meaningful alone time. Going to a place with no one else around for miles is, for me, helpful, but that might not be necessary for others.

Choosing your location

To reduce everyday distractions, it is useful wherever possible to get away from your normal living environment. Alternatively, you might visit your local park or forest. If you decide to remain at home or in your garden, you should try to go uninterrupted and undisturbed for a reasonable period. My feeling on this is to get away to somewhere you have not seen before, if at all possible.

Telling other people

The idea of us wanting to spend some time in solitude can be worrying to our loved ones in our lives if we suddenly announce our intentions. For example, partners can feel hurt and threatened if you declare a need for your own space, even if it is only for a short while. They may take it personally and wonder what it is they have done wrong to drive you away. It helps if you have previously discussed each other's views on what it means to be apart and to do your own thing in the context of your relationship. I am incredibly fortunate that my wife and family are always hugely supportive of what I want to do, even if it does appear to be somewhat wacky!

How to spend your time in solitude

Of course, you can simply go with the flow and do whatever you want, but you will get the most out of your special moments alone if you have a rough plan of things you want to achieve. For me, the first time I went into solitude, it most certainly had the ingredients of a project. I established a secure and dry base and then walked over the moor to rediscover places I walked in the Army many years earlier.

On Dartmoor, the plan sort of went according to how I thought it would, except I had not considered the effect of being alone really would have on me. After a week or so, I discovered that and I was drawn to walking specific paths given to me during dreamtime. I ended up walking for miles across the moor that I was not familiar with and without a map in rain, sun and at night. I also found that as time went on that, I felt the draw that nature had on me and its surroundings. I really fell in love with my surroundings.

Arrival ceremonies

On arrival, or as soon as possible, it is right and proper to hold a short ceremony honouring the land and space that you will be occupying as well as introducing yourself. Much of what I do know I owe to having attended such ceremonies with friends and my wife. This is what I do, but it is by no means a blueprint.

First of all, I will use my compass to ascertain the four cardinal directions. I will then face each in turn, starting with the East (where the sun will rise) and in turn, open my arms to that direction saying, "I come to you the East, bringer of all that comes from you, and ask for your blessings during my stay". Repeat this for each direction.

Now I turn my attention to heaven above and earth below. Again, with open arms stretched to the sky, proclaim your desire to the sky and heavens above. Repeat this to the planet (Gaia) below, sweeping your arms downwards and upwards to embrace your heart.

Something along the lines of "Oh Father Sky and Mother Earth, I ask for your blessings during my stay".

Now we have a circle which is your special place to move onto the next part. You can mark out your circle, for example, with some stones placed at the cardinal points or construct a mini stone or wooden circle all the way around. Whatever works for you and the physical space you have to work with is good enough.

I always like to enter my circle from the East, again from the direction of the rising sun. I will move around my circle in a clockwise direction and stop briefly to honour each cardinal point. I will walk around three times until then I move into the centre point. It is good to offer something to the earth from your home at the centre of the circle – water is often used, but it could also be stone or a piece of wood to place. Usually, I have used sacred water from holy wells or other parts of the world and gift this to the ground in the centre of the circle – again this, is a personal choice.

Now I can honour others. I will start by honouring the land and the spirits that roam the upper and lower kingdoms, the elementals (earth, fire, water and air), the inhabitants of the fairy worlds, every insect, bird and animal of the physical world, the plants and trees and the very ground that we walk on. All of these will be welcomed with something simple like, "I thank you ... for allowing me to share this space with you and feel honoured to be here at this and the places you roam".

A short time of reflection follows, and even a statement of intent might follow. "I am here in this beautiful space to reflect on who I truly am so that I can be more enlightened to the majesty of the world I inhabit".

Summary of Tips and Exercises

Tip	Exercise
1. Get outside.	1 – Go for a walk close to where you live and perhaps even across the fields or in a park. This time, however, make a conscious effort to slow down your walk. Make slower steps and look at what is around you. Be curious about the shape of trees, plants, spiders' webs. Look attentively at these objects and realise just how beautiful nature is.

2. Spend time on your outside.	2 – If you cannot spend days outside, then make an effort once a month to spend an entire day in perhaps a wood. Whilst you are there, you could even meditate. Most importantly, take notes on how it felt to be away from the hustle and bustle of everyday life. You will find it energising!
3. Study one aspect of nature over some time.	3 – Pick on an object in nature – it might be a sizeable prominent oak or a river or some hills. Sit somewhere to observe this item over the seasons and retake notes on seeing, sensing and feeling.

Chapter 9

Conclusion

Throughout this short book, we have travelled along a path to find positive thinking and happiness. It is true to say that we have a lot to do to achieve this, but the great and excellent news is that we can achieve all what we want! I believe it all comes down to a few small steps to attain self-confidence. This will ultimately lead to utilising all those things we have spoken about – our mental resilience, our mindfulness, our gratitude, our love of self. We may think we do not have the self-confidence to take on the world, nor should we. We just need to believe in ourselves. With that feel comes remarkable things for us and those around us.

How to Build Self-Confidence

I visited a good friend of mine the other day, and we were talking about confidence in young people. But then, this applies to adults as well. Some crazy statistics are going around currently, which, if true, tell us that well over three-quarters of all people suffer from a lack of self-confidence and self-esteem. This is turn, most definitely has an impact on happiness and success for so many people.

Self-confidence is the single, most important attribute to personal success.

It is one of the critical topics in self-development that is believed to be relevant to most people. This is not surprising since confidence is needed in every aspect of people's lives. A person would not be able to finish a race or perform on stage successfully without self-confidence.

Self-confidence is a state of being, a state of the mind and body, where a person believes in him/herself, what they can do, and what they can achieve. Without this self-belief, they cannot accomplish their dreams, or at least find it very difficult. If you believe it, it will have a good chance of coming true. For sure, if you do not think it, it will also be challenging to achieve.

Self-confidence is not only limited to one's beliefs.

It affects behaviour and actions. It affects the way a person moves and speaks. It involves the choices that a person makes. A self-confident woman's standard image is the one who stands tall, holds her head up high, and freely speaks her mind. She has an aura of positivity and optimism that affects the people she interacts with.

While this is true, self-confidence is also shown in other ways. A self-confident person also does the right thing even if he/she is criticised or ridiculed. A self-confident person is open to try new things and take on new opportunities. A self-confident person is humble enough to admit mistakes and accept compliments. Many successful leaders have self-confidence. People follow confident leaders and those that are sure of their cause or stand. It takes confidence to be a great leader.

A lot of self-development studies and articles have connected or linked self-confidence with success.

Confidence begets and leads to success.

Those who lack confidence or have low self-confidence struggle with success. Renowned author Brain Tracy says that those who believe in themselves can overcome barriers and do what it takes to succeed. He believes that real obstacles are in mind and not in the external or outside world. Winning internal battles is essential because it is a huge step to success.

Is confidence learned, or is it something that a person is born with? There are coaching and self-development articles, books and services that talk extensively about self-confidence. The fantastic news is that it can be learned and developed. Where do you start?

Well, it all starts in mind.

The first step is **self-assessment**. Take a good look at yourself – what you have done and what you have achieved so far. You have to know where you are to get to where you want to go. Part of self-assessment is to know your strengths and accepting your weaknesses. This is important because this can help you identify and anticipate future drawbacks and difficulties and help you avoid them.

The next step is **goal setting**. Plan, research and write down your goals. It is crucial to set deadlines since these will push you to get things done promptly and help you move to the next goal. Without deadlines, it would be easy to lose track of what you want to achieve.

Another essential step to building self-confidence is **managing your mind**.

Negative self-talk is counter-productive and may sabotage your chances of succeeding in life. People sabotage themselves all the time. They work hard to improve themselves; they read self-development books, get on a programme or set a specific course of action. Then after a while, they stop and go back to their old ways (the haunt of New Year's resolutions!). You can avoid this by having positive self-talk and by feeding your mind positivity and optimism.

Following the first three steps, it is time now to **commit**. Commit to your goals and consistently build habits that help you attain them. Write down any doubts that you have and challenge them rationally. Committing also provides motivation. It motivates you to stick to your goals despite difficulties and trials.

Sometimes, a person has low confidence because he/she lacks the knowledge or skills needed to accomplish a task. Increase your knowledge and skills by reading books and articles, attending courses and seminars, and attending coaching lessons.

It is essential though to start small. Start with your easy or small goals. Once you have achieved them, you can move on to bigger goals. Remember, a self-confident person gets out of his comfort zone and takes on new opportunities to learn and grow. In taking on new opportunities, he/she gains more chances and ways of succeeding.

As E.E. Cummings said, "once we believe in ourselves, we can risk curiosity, wonder, spontaneous delight, or any experience that reveals the human spirit".

Don't be afraid. Live and be self-confident and grasp the mantle of positive thought!

Disclaimer

This book contains opinions and ideas of the author and is meant to teach the reader informative and helpful knowledge while due care should be taken by the user in the application of the information provided. The instructions and strategies are possibly not right for every reader and there is no guarantee that they work for everyone. Using this book and implementing the information/recipes therein contained is explicitly your own responsibility and risk. This work with all its contents, does not guarantee correctness, completion, quality or correctness of the provided information. Misinformation or misprints cannot be completely eliminated.

Printed in Great Britain
by Amazon